Humanity Starts with You

11 Simple Rules
to Create Thriving Communities
for Children

D1597220

JUDY JABLON AND **NICHOLE PARKS**

Humanity Starts with You

Printed in the United States of America

First Printing, 2022

Leading for Children
71 South Orange Avenue, #356
South Orange, NJ 07079

www.leadingforchildren.org

Contents

Part 5

Simple Rules for
LEARNING EXPERIENCES

Part 6

Taking Action 148

Part 1

Welcome

Humanity Starts with You

How does a child cultivate an understanding of humanity? How do they learn kindness, empathy, and respect for others? Every individual must learn what it means to be human. And we know that early childhood is when this learning begins. We also know that it isn't what we say but what we do that matters most for children. They model our behavior.

Regardless of your role in a child's life, you help them learn to trust, explore, develop, and learn. There are so many ways your unique qualities matter for children. Your smile, sense of humor, the special sound of your voice, and the interests you share with children all contribute to how they understand the world around them. Everything they see in you and all the experiences and interactions they have with you significantly contribute to who they become. How you choose to be when you are around children—both your actions and your words—serves as a model for how to be in the world. You consistently send messages that shape how children see themselves, others, and the process of learning.

To thrive is to flourish, it is to bloom. For a child, it means that they are able to meet their potential, to be happy, healthy, joyful, curious, and strong.

—Joan Lombardi

As the adults in children's lives, we have the ability and responsibility to ensure that children thrive. While this is a sacred trust, it's not without challenges. It's hard to consistently be the responsive, encouraging partner that children need. The daily care of young children, whether as a caregiver, parent, family member, or educator, can be tiring and sometimes overwhelming. In addition, systemic inequities, crises of conflict, climate change, and COVID-19 have greatly exacerbated some of the challenges the adults in children's lives face each day. Many of us go to bed each night worrying and wondering.

Are you, like so many of us, struggling to find the resilience needed to be fully present and intentional with children as you constantly pivot and respond to changes around you? Whether it's navigating a patchwork of care and support for your child so you can go to work; making decisions about virtual or in-person learning; or supporting the social emotional development of your child, we're seeing that the resilience of families has been stretched in unprecedented ways across all demographics.

Are you, like so many educators of young children in settings everywhere, navigating your own family life and at the same time trying to show up effectively at work for children, families, and colleagues? Perhaps you're struggling to make a living wage by holding two jobs and still effectively providing exemplary care and education. The field of early learning is rife with declining morale, anxiety, exhaustion, and depression. As educators, many of us are living in a state of stress.

Yet research and years of experience show that we have capacities we can harness and strengthen. We can empower ourselves to act with intention even in difficult circumstances. To realize this, we must work together. When we unite as partners to be our best for children, we can lighten each other's burdens. We can no longer afford the status quo of hierarchies, siloed roles, and inequitable power structures that create tension and dissonance, nullifying efforts for true collaboration. We have to create systems that bring us together to strengthen one another and ensure that children thrive.

We know that strong adults make strong children, and this leads to thriving communities. Encouraging kindness, empathy, and respect for others are urgent tasks and are our only path toward a better future. Listening to each other is not extracurricular. It's not just a nice thing to do. Humanity is not a lofty idea; it's the heart of our daily life. It's how we treat one another. It's everything we say and do, and it's what children experience and learn from every day. Building our humanity is fulfilling our true potential. It's a necessity, not an option. And it's not only for some of us, but for all of us. Humanity starts with you.

We invite you to harness your power and join us as leaders for children! We must come together and support each other to ensure that children can develop and learn in settings where they feel safe and secure. This requires all the important adults in children's lives to share an understanding of what children need to thrive so that we can collectively apply it across all spaces where children live.

At the center of our coming together must be equity and respect for all. Children cannot thrive within systems that favor one child over another, nor can they thrive surrounded by socially constructed silos. For children to truly thrive, we must celebrate the humanity of each individual. This means changing the zero-sum thinking that what's good for one group has to come at the expense of another. This is an imperative to achieving equity. Now is the time to tap into our wisdom and experience, and forge equitable partnerships for each other and for our children. We can create cultures of shared learning and decision making within our communities.

A critical first step to achieving equity is to start inclusive conversations among adults. In this book, *11 Simple Rules to Create Thriving Communities for Children*, we offer a path to this shared understanding. During the past few years, we have seen

what occurs when communities of adults come together and engage in authentic dialogue about their vision for children. In Mississippi, our colleagues have used the 11 Simple Rules framework to strengthen relationships between families and childcare centers and foster collaboration among educators in childcare centers. In Wyoming, the 11 Simple Rules ignited conversations among adults with very different roles within the young child's ecosystem, and the result is a new statewide vision of what children need to thrive that guided the development of Wyoming's early-learning standards.

Imagine our communities as places where all relationships and interactions among adults and children are honest, open, trusting, and two-way. Where our environments— our homes, workplaces, parks, libraries, or early-learning programs—are safe, calm, organized, and respectful. Where adults and children together learn with and from each other in ways that are meaningful, exploratory, and actionable. How would that feel? How would it feel for you? How might it feel for children?

About the Book

We invite you to use the 11 Simple Rules to support you and your community in establishing a shared vision of quality relationships and interactions, environments, and learning experiences. We hope you will use it as the basis for inclusive conversations that build on the strengths, wisdom, and experience within your community.

This book is written for all the adults within the child's ecosystem. Whether you are a family member, community leader, or kitchen manager in an early-learning program, we hope this book provides inspiration and insight, and promotes a deeper understanding of your impact on the lives of children. While it can be used individually as a learning and self-reflection tool, we hope that you will use it to ignite collaborative conversations, learning, and growth.

The book is organized into six parts. You are reading Part 1, which we hope is welcoming you and providing a summary of our goals for this book. Part 2 is an overview of the 11 Simple Rules framework. Parts 3, 4, and 5 describe the rules in detail. We have organized the rules according to three categories—relationships and interactions, the emotional and physical environment, and learning experiences—because these are important aspects of what helps children to thrive. We offer an in-depth exploration of each simple rule using photos, examples, reflective questions, and research findings substantiating its importance. In Part 6, we invite you to take action, to be a change agent and a leader for children. We offer tools to support you in conversations with others in your community to implement the 11 Simple Rules. Finally, we have included a comprehensive list of references organized by the rules at the end of the book.

We believe this book will help us achieve equity in all our actions, interactions, and throughout our environments. As you read the 11 Simple Rules and talk about them with others, strive to share language, understanding, and intention about how to be with children and each other. And as you use the 11 Simple Rules day to day, cultivate self-awareness in order to be purposeful about your actions with and on behalf of children.

We have a fierce passion to make a difference in children's lives. If you have chosen to pick up this book, we believe you share our passion. Let's work together to put humanity first for our children.

Judy and Nichole

~ Part 2 ~

The 11 Simple Rules Framework

We initially conceived of the 11 Simple Rules as a way to ensure quality early learning for young children, creating a safe and nurturing environment while promoting their physical, social, emotional, and intellectual development. However, we quickly recognized two important ideas that have influenced the thinking in this book: 1) these simple rules apply to all spaces where children spend time, and 2) they also apply to adults and can create a healthier climate for everyone. When adults thrive, children have a better chance to thrive!

Accessible to all and replicable in any setting, the 11 Simple Rules are organized into three important categories that are easy to remember and uncomplicated to talk about.

Relationships and interactions that are honest, open, trusting, and two-way.

Emotional and physical environments that are safe, calm, organized, and respectful.

Learning experiences that are meaningful, exploratory, and actionable.

HONEST, OPEN, TRUSTING, *and* TWO-WAY

We know that our relationships and interactions powerfully affect children's learning, emotional well-being, and even their physical health, today and in the future. When children are surrounded by a web of positive relationships, and when they experience interactions with people they trust who validate, encourage, and challenge them, they flourish. They also develop the skills to handle adversity when it inevitably comes their way. Children's interactions with warm, sensitive, responsive adults literally wire children's brains for success in life. It's also true that adults benefit from strong positive relationships with other adults. Relationships help us feel a sense of belonging, support our overall health, and reduce stress.

Interactions that convey the message "I care about you" lead to strong, trusting relationships.

Listen for the "I care" message in these examples:

- *Gently rubbing Susie's back as she settles down for a nap.*
- *Saying good morning to Amelia, your co-teacher, as she enters the classroom.*

- *Leaning in toward Derek, a child in your class, as you sit together on the floor while he tells you about his new puppy.*
- *Saying to Philippe, "Thank you for helping Sam open his milk."*
- *Snuggling with your child as you read a bedtime story together.*
- *Bringing extra bottles of water to work for your colleagues.*

Each example highlights how we demonstrate caring for someone. In the first years of a child's life, feeling nurtured and cared for contributes to the development of healthy brain architecture. Children develop and learn through strong positive relationships and interactions with all the adults who care for them. Relationships and learning go hand in hand. For adults and children, how we feel when we are with another person affects our ability to think and learn.

❖ *Think about how you feel when you are with someone you care about. Are you relaxed? Comfortable? Safe?*

In contrast, think about what it's like to be with someone who makes you feel uncertain, on edge, or defensive.

Children watch us all the time. The adults in children's lives are the most powerful models for learning how to be with others. When children are surrounded by relationships and interactions among adults that are healthy and strong, they thrive.

❖ *Take time to reflect and add examples of your relationships and interactions.*

Simple Rules for the Emotional and Physical Environment

SAFE, CALM, ORGANIZED,
and RESPECTFUL

Are you someone who pays close attention to your surroundings? It turns out we're actually very sensitive to our environment, which affects how we feel, how we relate to others, and our ability to focus on tasks.

Picture for a moment an airy, light-filled space. Now visualize a cluttered room without windows. These are physical characteristics of the environment. As you imagine being in either of these two spaces, what happens to your mood? The physical environment and the emotional environment are hard to pull apart. One affects the other.

The physical environment is the space itself, including the light, colors, furniture, temperature, and whether indoors or outside. The emotional environment is the atmosphere and climate of the space. Are people relaxed? Are they arguing? We feel the mood of the environment. It can be light and easy or heavy and unpleasant.

Yes, the emotional and physical environments are different, but because they are so interrelated, we present them together. The hum of the air conditioner or the quick glances between two people can fade into the background as we go about our day, or they can affect our well-being and cause stress. A calm and aesthetic environment can enhance our mood and help us to relax. These aspects of the physical and emotional environment also affect how children feel—their stress level, attentiveness, social interactions, even their ability to remember.

As the adults in children's lives, how we feel in a particular space also influences how children respond. We can become irritable for no apparent reason in a very noisy room, or we might become anxious when we feel disrespected. Perhaps we perk up a bit and smile at the smell of a delicious lunch arriving. And our irritability or pleasure is infectious. If we're grumpy, children notice. When we're upbeat, they notice that too. The environment can work for us or against us. When we recognize the impact of the environment on children and adults, we can actively shape surroundings that help everyone thrive.

Notice the decisions adults make about the emotional and physical environment to support everyone's well-being:

- *Before the infants in her program arrive each morning, Tiffany checks the classroom for potential hazards by lying on the floor to get a child's-eye view.*

- *Daphne, a center director, has a table and chairs in her office for conversations with families and staff rather than sitting across from them at her desk.*

- *At the end of a long day, Max, the after-school teacher, brings the children outdoors to sit beside the river and listen to the sounds in nature.*

- *Brian, father of three, plays the song "The Final Countdown" to invite his children to tidy up their playroom.*

- *In Valerie's family childcare home, she has soft lighting and pastel colors in the playroom to create a calm, inviting space.*

- *Chue regularly checks his son's car seat to ensure that it is correctly installed.*

The examples above illustrate how adults make decisions that influence how both adults and children experience the emotional and physical environment. Calm, organized spaces help us focus and relax. Noisy, cluttered spaces with poor lighting and air circulation can increase stress and anxiety.

❖ *Think about spaces you enter that relax you, help you calm down, and encourage you to focus. What are some qualities of these spaces?*

Think about spaces you enter that make you anxious, create distractions, or cause you stress. What are some qualities of these spaces?

In settings for children's learning, carefully designed spaces make it easy for children to explore safely and independently while comfortable and engaged. When families feel welcomed when they arrive at their child's program, they feel more relaxed and secure leaving their child to go about their day. When staff members come to work, a friendly and attractive environment sets everyone up to have a productive and satisfying day.

Four simple rules guide our decision making when we plan a healthy, equitable, emotional and physical environment: it is safe, calm, organized, and respectful. These rules together set the stage for effective relationships, interactions, and learning. We can use the simple rules as a tool for thinking together about how we can create spaces where everyone experiences safety, calm, order, and respect from the moment they walk in the door. When we think about environments that promote well-being for adults and children, they must be free from hazards and dangers, while also allowing each person to feel empowered, respected, and excited to learn.

❖ *Take time to reflect and add examples of the emotional and physical environments where you spend time.*

Simple Rules for Learning Experiences

MEANINGFUL, EXPLORATORY,
and ACTIONABLE

When we encounter something new, we learn. We find out some new bit of information, consider a new idea, think differently about something we already know, or learn and practice a new skill. These are all learning experiences. We invite you to think about this for children and for adults. Perhaps we decide to plant a garden, fix a broken appliance, buy a new phone, or try a new recipe. We are powerful models of curiosity, investigation, and problem solving for children, who are learning new things all the time. Learning experiences activate curiosity and encourage us to wonder, stretch our thinking, and discover new things.

Learning experiences happen throughout the day:

- *Two-year-old Alang tilts his head toward the sky and feels the breeze dance across his face.*
- *While fishing with her family, five-year-old Benu gently holds a tadpole in her hand to examine how it moves.*

- *Cecilia, a kitchen manager, suggests that the children in Ms. Luanne's preschool classroom help her pick vegetables from the program's garden.*

- *Ryan, a program director, sits quietly and observes Kaleo, a teacher of two-year-olds, as he reads the group a story. Ryan captures two photos and a brief video to share with Kaleo so they can observe and describe the children's responses in their conversation later that day.*

- *Xiu, a three-year-old, claps her hands as her friend Tamara taps the drum with delight.*

- *Six-month-old Mateo pumps his legs in excitement when he hears the sound the ball makes as his foot connects with it.*

Each of these examples illustrates how curiosity ignites the opportunity for a learning experience. Sometimes learning experiences are spontaneous and other times they are planned.

Adults and children benefit when learning experiences build on existing knowledge or experiences and invite them to extend their thinking in a way that is the perfect balance of safety and risk. We offer three simple rules for learning experiences: they are meaningful, exploratory, and actionable.

When learning experiences are meaningful, they're relevant to the learner. For example, Lori is about to welcome a child to her class who is arriving from Pakistan. She finds it meaningful to do some online research to familiarize herself with the country and the culture of Pakistan. When learning experiences are exploratory, the learner gets to mess around. Dave and his daughter Addie are building castles on the sand. They explore how wet the sand has to be for the castles to be sturdy. When learning experiences are actionable, you can turn around and use what you learn in a practical way. Reading a recipe to make muffins leads right to baking them and having a tasty treat! When learning experiences are meaningful, exploratory, and actionable, learning is satisfying and enjoyable, which makes adults and children want to learn more.

❖ *Think about a recent learning experience you had that was enjoyable. What happened? Were you alone? With a partner? What made you curious and ignited your learning?*

Think about a learning experience you had either recently or in the past that you found frustrating or unsatisfying. Can you identify the reasons why?

Take time to reflect and add examples of learning experiences that ignite your curiosity.

The 11 Simple Rules Are Guideposts

As you think about the 11 Simple Rules, we hope you can quickly visualize each one. For example, think about a two-way interaction. When have you experienced a satisfying two-way conversation? What qualities did the exchange have? How might you create these qualities in your future interactions?

At their core, the 11 Simple Rules are guideposts and reminders. They're not prescriptions for behavior. Instead, they describe the essential elements of quality—what children and adults need to be comfortable with each other and to grow and learn. They are easy to keep in mind as you go about your day. When you encounter an unexpected situation or a stressful interaction, the 11 Simple Rules offer an invitation to pause, think, and act with intention. We believe you'll find examples of the simple rules in your homes, programs, and communities. Throughout the book you'll find lots of photos and stories that show the simple rules in action.

The 11 Simple Rules Framework Promotes Greater Equity

The 11 Simple Rules are accessible to every adult in the child's ecosystem, such as family members, teachers, directors, van drivers, kitchen staff, librarians, recreation staff, and mayors. They can contribute to meaningful conversations about how to be together, what spaces can look like, and how learning experiences can be successful. People bring their unique experiences as the group constructs shared meaning about each rule and how it shows up day to day. Everyone can relate and contribute to the conversation.

When we began developing the 11 Simple Rules, it was in partnership with members of the early-learning community. Rather than a top-down approach that said "This is what quality looks like," we asked members of our Learning Networks to think of elements of quality they observed in their own settings. Each group looked for common themes, and we collectively arrived at the set of terms that became the 11 Simple

Rules. These rules are accessible to all and replicable in any setting, whether an early-learning program, a recreation center, a workplace for adults, or your home.

The 11 Simple Rules framework provides coherence—a logical and consistent way for everyone, regardless of their individual role, to understand and talk about quality. As we define what quality means in early learning, it's crucial for all of us to be on the same page or, as we say, sing from the same song sheet. When we describe quality in clear, concise words, we paint a picture in our minds. This is critical to making quality tangible and achievable. The simple rules foster a shared understanding among all the adults in children's lives and encourage them to take an active role in creating quality for children.

Children thrive on consistency. A unique feature of the 11 Simple Rules framework is that it includes definitions that apply to children and adults. They represent multiple viewpoints to ensure that everyone's experience is shared: adult with adult, adult with child, and child with child. Simply put, what we're asking adults to do with and for children is the same as what we should do with and for each other.

While we believe that the 11 Simple Rules put us on a path to equity, we acknowledge that we're working in a context of deep inequities in access and outcomes, especially for children of color and children from underresourced communities. While the 11 Simple Rules framework on its own cannot comprehensively address this situation, it can help facilitate consistent, quality practice among all adults in the child's ecosystem.

Not only do the 11 Simple Rules support learning and development for all children; they also create settings for adults that are safe and responsive to each person's needs. The impact? Adults feel respected, supported, and effective within their community. They are intentional about respecting and supporting others. They are the foundation for thriving communities for all and provide models of action and interaction that children will take into their futures.

Part 3

Simple Rules for Relationships and Interactions

Healthy relationships and interactions begin with you!

Four simple rules guide our decision making as we engage in strong, positive relationships and interactions: they are HONEST, OPEN, TRUSTING, and TWO-WAY. These four simple rules together lay the foundation for equity and respect in relationships and interactions.

Honest

Be honest in your relationships and interactions.

Honest means genuine, truthful, and not deceptive. When you choose to be honest in relationships and interactions, you let others get to know the real you—your authentic and sincere self. When you're honest in relationships, you communicate a true desire to know another person and a willingness to let them know you. At the same time, being honest doesn't mean telling everything about yourself. Sometimes we keep things to ourselves to preserve boundaries or to avoid causing hurt or embarrassment to another person.

Sincere, genuine, authentic, transparent

❖ *What words or phrases come to mind as you think about honest relationships and interactions?*

Ms. Marneshia and Ms. Gina sit side by side in honest conversation. Their willingness to be genuine and transparent with each other sets the tone for a positive program climate. What do you notice that conveys to you that Ms. Marneshia and Ms. Gina are having an honest interaction?

Understanding Honest Relationships and Interactions

How do we create honest relationships and interactions? We're authentic and truthful. As you read these stories, notice what the simple rule of honesty looks like day to day.

IN THE WORKPLACE

Sarah and Maria are close friends who work at the community family resource center. Recently, Maria was promoted to site manager. As the site manager, she is now part of the leadership team responsible for making decisions and guiding the direction of the center. During a dinner together, Sarah asks Maria about a recent leadership meeting. Maria pauses as she navigates her feelings about Sarah's questions. She wants things to be comfortable between the two of them, but she also knows it would be unprofessional to discuss leadership conversations. She hadn't thought about how her promotion could change the dynamics of her friendship. Maria says, "Sarah, I know we usually tell each other everything and it feels weird not to be able to discuss certain things with you. It's also important to me that I maintain professional integrity. I can't discuss those conversations with you. Thank you for respecting that." By being honest about how she was experiencing the conversation, Maria was able to convey healthy boundaries.

IN A CHILDCARE SETTING

Liana, a four-year-old with hearing loss, is new to Dominique's classroom at Springdale Elementary School. On the first day of school, Liana's parents, Mia and Liko, demonstrate how to manage Liana's hearing aids and ask Dominique to wear an assistive amplification device. Dominique accepts the technology, and the parents say goodbye. Dominique is nervous. She's never used this equipment before and while Liana's parents have described to her how it works, she doesn't feel comfortable. Dominique is committed to being honest, so at the end of the day, she asks Liana's parents to show her how to use the technology again. The next morning, Mia and Liko arrive smiling. They express their gratitude to Dominique, saying, "Thank you so much for asking us! In the past, we've just dropped Liana off at school, crossed our fingers, and hoped she can hear what she needs to learn." Going forward, Dominique and Liana's parents have regular conversations at drop-off. As weeks pass, Mia and Liko notice that Liana is smiling when she gets home and speaking about her new friends. Dominique's honesty about her discomfort and desire to learn more allowed her to gain the knowledge necessary to support Liana, while also building trust with Liana's parents.

❖ *What did you find interesting as you read about honesty in action?*

Think about a recent interaction you had that was honest. What made it so?

Choose one story to think about. How might things have turned out if the person didn't choose to be honest?

Why Do Honest Relationships and Interactions Matter?

When relationships and interactions are honest, people are willing to be transparent and vulnerable in a respectful way. They send the message "I'm real with you and it's safe for you to be real with me." Humans need to feel a sense of belonging, to be valued and supported. Research shows that when we're honest in our personal and professional lives, we're more likely to have relationships that meet this fundamental need. Sometimes being honest means delivering news that is hard to hear. Being kind in what and how you choose to share is really important so that you preserve the relationship.

RESEARCH TELLS US

Honest relationships and interactions strengthen connections. When we're honest, what we're thinking and feeling internally matches how we act and behave with others. This conveys that we're dependable. Others know what to expect from us. When expectations between people are clear, there is less anxiety about what we say and do. When people have honest communication and authentic interpersonal interactions at home and at work they tend to be less stressed and more relaxed.

Honest relationships and interactions lead to more honesty. Honest relationships and interactions are contagious. Adults who are honest in their interactions with other adults are modeling honesty for children. When adults are honest with children, they also encourage children to behave with honesty. Honest interactions lead to stronger connections, and with each honest interaction, the effects ripple outward.

Honest relationships and interactions encourage collaboration and problem solving. When others are honest with us, we are more likely to adjust to change. We are more open to discussing and learning from our mistakes. When others around us are honest, it's easier to work together to seek solutions. We approach challenges with a clear and shared understanding of how we can work together and learn from each other. We are less likely to find ourselves caught in power struggles. Honest relationships and interactions enhance our ability to face challenges and solve problems.

❖ *As you consider the research about honest relationships and interactions, what feels important to you?*

Honest Relationships and Interactions in Communities

We invite you to observe the honest relationships and interactions shared by our partners in communities near and far.

A small group of children have gathered outdoors for a serious, honest conversation. They have been reading a book about race and belonging, and the children are eager to share their feelings.

Observe the genuine emotions of this teacher-child interaction. When children can express their true and honest feelings with their teachers, they learn to trust and are more open to learning.

It's a moment of big-sister honesty as Adelaide tells her little brother, Solomon, how much she loves playing with him.

❖ Invitation to Explore

Think of someone you know who makes it easy for you to be honest and authentic. What qualities do they possess that help you feel that way? Do you share any of them?

Think about a connection you have that you would like to strengthen. When might you see them next? Could you arrange a chat? Set an intention to pause and think about how you want to check in.

Simple Rule #2

Open

Stay open in your relationships and interactions.

Open means approachable. Being open in relationships and interactions expands our thinking, our willingness to consider new ideas, and helps us acknowledge what we don't know. You listen to learn, to avoid judgments, to ask questions, and to seek to understand others on a deeper level. An open attitude affects how you connect with others.

Approachable, vulnerable, nonjudgmental, accessible, welcoming

❖ *What words come to mind when you think about open relationships and interactions?*

39

Ms. Sylvester, program owner and director, greets families each morning as they drop off their children. As she and Ms. Roberta chat briefly, Ms. Sylvester wants to convey that she is approachable and accessible to families so parents know their child is safe and secure. What do you notice that conveys to you an open interaction?

❖ *What do you notice that conveys to you an open interaction?*

Understanding Open Relationships and Interactions

What does it mean to have an open relationship and interaction? You decide to be approachable and not to judge. As you read these stories, notice what open relationships and interactions look like day to day.

AT HOME

It's important to Paul and Patrick that their five-year-old daughter, Pearl, grows up in a household that celebrates diversity. They often wonder what Pearl's experience is like at school and whether she feels singled out as the only child with two dads. Paul is good at staying open. He asks Pearl about her school day when she comes home, and when families are invited to visit the class, he shares baby pictures of Pearl. Patrick has some unresolved concerns. His biggest fear is that she'll be bullied or made fun of. He partners with Paul to learn more by setting up a conference with Pearl's teacher, Belinda. By being open about their family structure, Patrick and Paul are helping their daughter to be more successful at school, forging a partnership with Pearl's teacher, and modeling for Pearl the importance of openness and transparency.

IN A CHILDCARE SETTING

Roxanne was having a hard time communicating with Zion's family. When she asked Cheri, Zion's mother, if she would like Zion to participate in the lunch program at the center, Cheri said no and appeared upset. Roxanne spoke with Margaret, her program's director, about Cheri's reaction. Margaret said, "Zion's family is Muslim. Perhaps they have specific dietary requirements. Zion brings his own lunch every day." This prompted Roxanne to study the center menus, and she realized there were several dishes that were not appropriate to a Muslim diet. When she next saw Cheri, Roxanne said, "I noticed that the center's menus are not appropriate for a Muslim diet. I am wondering if you could give us some suggestions to change the menu so that Zion could have the center lunch?" Cheri smiled broadly.

"Thank you so much for noticing. I'm happy you understand." Roxanne realized that staying open and not shutting down in response to Cheri's reactions improved their relationship and strengthened their partnership to support Zion. As a result, Zion feels more comfortable at school.

❖ *What did you find interesting in the examples in action?*

Think about a recent interaction you had that was open. What made it so?

Why Do Open Relationships and Interactions Matter?

When we're open, we're curious to learn more about experiences, ideas, and people. This helps us question and discover new dimensions to our beliefs. We might also think in new ways about past decisions and mistakes. Staying open to new information can help us adapt more quickly to change. When we model openness for children, we support them to become resilient, competent, and confident adults.

RESEARCH TELLS US

Open relationships and interactions help us adapt to changing circumstances. When we're open, we're curious to learn more about experiences and ideas. We ask questions, consider alternative perspectives, and expand our beliefs. We think in new ways about past decisions and mistakes. Staying open to new information allows us to adapt more quickly to change and to be resilient. As a result, we have a greater sense of well-being and can more quickly recover from trouble or distress.

Open relationships and interactions encourage us to reach out to others. An open attitude motivates us to learn more about other people and different ways of life. We gain appreciation for diverse perspectives and sensitivity to other cultures. Our openness can influence others. Showing curiosity about another person's perspective can encourage them to keep thinking, questioning, and refining their ideas.

Open relationships and interactions help us learn together. The ways family members show openness and curiosity affect how children learn. When parents and caregivers are more open to new ideas, the children in their care tend to be more joyful, responsive, and willing to engage in other positive behaviors. Openness in adults encourages children to reach out to their families, caregivers, and peers.

Cultivating open relationships and interactions helps us better appreciate what each of us has to offer as we navigate the challenges of providing for our children and programs. When we embrace a culture of openness, we model for children that all voices matter and deserve respect. In turn, children grow up knowing that their thoughts and feelings matter and that being open with others leads to respectful relationships.

❖ *As you consider the research about open relationships and interactions, what feels important to you?*

Open Relationships and Interactions in Communities

Notice open relationships and interactions shared by our partners in communities near and far.

Ms. Mimi sits on the bench with the children as they watch other friends dance across the room. This open and easy moment of laughter and joy helps to strengthen their relationships.

Enola and her daughter, Kimi, are enjoying a relaxed and joyful walk in the park, treasuring this special time together. Experimenting with language, Kimi says, "Look Mama. It's birding." They stop and look, laughing openly with delight.

Ms. Mona invites Mrs. Randolf, a parent of a child in her classroom, to have an open conversation about an email Mrs. Randolf sent earlier that day. By talking together, they easily resolve a misunderstanding. When the adults in children's lives work together in real and genuine ways, children thrive.

❖ Invitation to Explore

Think of the people you know. Who would you describe as open in a way that is comfortable for you? What qualities do they demonstrate that convey openness to you?

Often a thought partner is a helpful way to reflect on qualities of relationships and interactions. Who might be a good thought partner for you to continue exploring the idea of being open in relationships and interactions?

Simple Rule #3

◆

Trusting

Foster trusting relationships and interactions.

Trusting means sincere and accepting. When relationships and interactions are trusting, you can count on others, and they can count on you. Trust is a feeling that develops in response to the actions and words of someone else. Trusting relationships and interactions are safe and comfortable, and you each know you're there to support the other.

Sincere, reliable, dependable, unquestioning

❖ *What words come to mind when you think about trusting relationships and interactions?*

As Martiza reads with her grandchild, three-year-old Gaia rests her head on her chest. She knows her grandma is here for her and that she can relax with her. This interaction helps Gaia feel secure as she learns to love listening to stories. What do you notice in this photo that conveys a trustworthy relationship?

Understanding Trusting Relationships and Interactions

What does trusting look like for you? When someone is willing to support you and is sincere and dependable, a trusting relationship can grow. Notice how trusting shows up in these examples.

IN THE WORKPLACE

Stephen, a dad of two children under three, is an employee at a grocery store in the Midwest. He's responsible for dropping the children off at their childcare program before work. Michaela, Stephen's supervisor, asks if he can begin coming in an hour earlier due to staff shortages. Stephen wants to show up for his team, but he also knows that it will be impossible for him to come in that early. He takes a deep breath and says, "Michaela, I know this recent staffing shortage has been hard. I want to pitch in. I can't come in early during the week because I take my children to school. Are there any other gaps in the schedule that I could help with?" Michaela asks if Stephen could work later in the day. Together, they look at the schedule and find a solution. Stephen trusts Michaela to understand his commitment to the store and to his family. Michaela trusts that she can rely on Stephen.

IN A CHILDCARE SETTING

Fatuma is a four-year-old with strong emotions. Daniela, her teacher, is ready to help Fatuma navigate challenges. Daniela hears Fatuma scream, "No, Siham!" Before she can get to where the two children are playing, Fatuma knocks over the structure they are building. Siham, looking upset, sits down and begins to reassemble the pieces. Daniela invites Fatuma to a quiet part of the classroom, where they sit together. Daniela calms herself so that she can help calm Fatuma as well. Daniela suggests that they take deep breaths together. Fatuma's breathing slows down and her body relaxes. Through Daniela's steady and repeated support, Fatuma knows that she can trust her teacher when strong emotions arise.

❖ *What did you find interesting in the examples in action?*

Think about a recent interaction you had that was trusting. What made it so?

Colleagues Thomas and Cynthia use sign language to discuss their day as they walk home together after work.

Why Do Trusting Relationships and Interactions Matter?

Building and maintaining trust has many positive benefits in our relationships and interactions with others. When we trust the people around us, we feel more secure, more willing to engage, and better prepared to tackle the challenges that come our way. When people trust us, they are more likely to be open to our ideas and can relax and learn with us.

RESEARCH TELLS US

Trusting relationships and interactions help us learn and grow. Children feel safe and cared for when they trust you. This is true for adults as well. Trust is the foundation for development and learning. When we interact with those we trust, we're more open and relaxed in learning and sharing ideas. We're also more comfortable accepting new experiences and are curious to see what will happen.

Trusting relationships and interactions strengthen our support networks. When we trust those around us, we feel more secure and motivated to participate in group activities and build stronger social bonds. When we feel trusted, we are more likely to trust others in return. This contributes to mutual respect and open communication, and it encourages shared decision making. We feel free to be ourselves, to rely and depend on each other, and to share our experiences at deeper levels.

Trusting relationships and interactions inspire us to act in our communities. When we feel trusted, we're more likely to be actively involved in our communities. We're confident that others will value our participation. Sharing in a culture of trust allows strangers to connect more quickly. This creates opportunities for learning and growth.

When the quality of our adult interactions improves, children benefit. As leaders for children at home and at school, we can be intentional about what we model for them. When our interactions with each other are trusting and authentic, children learn to relate to their peers, caregivers, and family members in that same way. When trust is present, it makes all our work easier.

❖ *As you consider the research about trustworthy relationships and interactions, what feels important to you?*

Trusting Relationships and Interactions in Communities

Notice trusting relationships and interactions shared by our partners in communities near and far.

Brittany has been watching other children play on the swings for several days, but wasn't ready to take a turn. Today, Ms. Lucia invites Brittany to give it a try, and together they share a trusting moment of delight.

Five-month-old Genevieve is learning to trust the water in the secure arms of her dad. They are blowing kisses to each other.

Eleven-month-old Noah learns about trust as his mom holds him safely in her arms. This sweet dog is blind, and Noah wants to pet him.

❖ Invitation to Explore

Explore how the simple rule of trusting shows up in your relationships and interactions with children, families, and colleagues.

Partner with others to explore how it feels to have trusting relationships and interactions.

Two-Way

Strive for two-way relationships and interactions.

Two-way means mutual and reciprocal. Relationships and interactions that are two-way are balanced and based on communication where each person listens and contributes so that the feeling is equitable. Two-way relationships and interactions allow for collaboration and mutual problem solving.

Reciprocal, mutual, back-and-forth, collaborative

❖ *What words come to mind when you think about two-way relationships and interactions?*

Ted and his son, Win, exchange smiles, words, and laughter. This two-way interaction helps Win learn about relationships and communication. What do you notice in this photo that conveys two-way to you?

Understanding Two-Way Relationships and Interactions

Most of us have had interactions that are one-way; one person just talks and talks. A two-way interaction involves real back-and-forth. Whether this develops in the moment or over time, a two-way relationship is equitable and more satisfying. As you read these stories, notice what two-way relationships and interactions look like.

AT HOME

Darian's separated parents, Crystal and Derrick, work well as a team and successfully manage Darian's transition between households. To make sure communication is consistent, they email back and forth about specifics. Whenever Crystal or Derrick talks about the other parent to Darian, their remarks are respectful and pleasant. When changes affect Darian's school experience, such as bringing an overnight bag for the weekend on a Friday, one parent always sends an email to the teacher and copies the other. Crystal and Derrick's co-parenting relationship is balanced, and their two-way interactions ensure that Darian has an easygoing and positive relationship with both parents.

IN A CHILDCARE SETTING

Evan is a newer four-year-old child in Karri's preschool class. Karri notices that during arrival Evan often cries as he approaches the classroom, hides behind his dad's legs, and struggles to say goodbye. Javier, Evan's dad, looks distressed in the mornings, and their drop-off time has grown later and later. Karri calls Javier to discuss Evan's difficulty separating. Javier describes how hard it has been to get Evan to school and expresses his relief that Karri has called. They discuss mutual strategies to support Evan as he transitions from home to school. After several days of working together, they notice that Evan no longer cries as he approaches the classroom, and drop-off is quicker. Karri and Javier's two-way relationship, where each shared and listened, enabled them to create a solution that responded to Evan's needs.

❖ *What did you find interesting in the examples in action?*

  Think about a recent interaction you had that was two-way. What made it so?

Why Do Two-Way Relationships and Interactions Matter?

When relationships and interactions are two-way, there is an even exchange and there is space and value for the thoughts and ideas of all involved. In an ideal two-way interaction, both people feel seen and heard. Research has shown reciprocal relationships are more positive and respectful and lead to more satisfying interactions. Two-way relationships allow us to feel more genuinely connected to the people in our lives.

Too often, our relationships involve unequal power dynamics and hierarchical relationships that undermine effectiveness and present unhealthy models for children. Even when there is a difference in roles and power, we can strive for two-way relationships and interactions and more effective communication.

RESEARCH TELLS US

Two-way relationships increase our satisfaction and success. When our relationships are two-way, adults feel more satisfied in work and children experience better outcomes in school. We feel more connected to the people in our lives, and we have space to share ideas and offer support.

Two-way relationships break down power imbalances. Two-way communication and mutual understanding can help bring balance to hierarchical relationships. In our workplaces, for example, when employees feel that their bosses genuinely listen to their concerns and trust them to make important decisions, the employees are happier in their roles. With children, offering choices and welcoming dialogue about possible actions gives them a sense of agency. Children feel that they are problem solvers and decision makers. When they feel seen and heard, they develop independence and confidence.

Two-way relationships build stronger communities. The impact of two-way relationships can extend beyond the interpersonal. A study found that parents who were engaged in strong two-way friendships, for example, more readily found ways to collaboratively support and work together to nurture their children. Their reciprocal interactions laid the groundwork for networks of support. In two-way relationships between parents and children, interactive play helped children develop stronger social skills and more positive interactions with other children their age. They model the collaborative behavior they see from the adults in their lives.

Two-way relationships and interactions require us to be fully present. When we are present, the other person is more likely to be as well. When we take time to think and create space for each other, we have more satisfying interactions. We also model respectful interactions for children. Finally, fostering two-way relationships helps us unlock the intelligence and wisdom of those we interact with, whether children or adults.

❖ *As you consider the research about two-way relationships and interactions, what feels important to you?*

Two-Way Relationships and Interactions in Communities

Notice two-way relationships and interactions shared by our partners in communities near and far.

Elijah is working on a greeting card to give to his mom and can't wait to tell Ms. Esther, his teacher, about it. When she sits down to listen, they exchange a playful laugh when he tells her how he is folding the paper so that it pops out of the envelope.

Mrs. DePaul and Jayla take turns reading together, going back and forth with each page. Sometimes they read the words and other times they chat about the pictures. This relaxed exchange strengthens their bond and encourages Jayla to take more risks as a reader.

As Miranda holds the book, Skylar tells the story, using some words and the pictures. Together they enjoy some quiet time in the classroom.

❖ Invitation to Explore

Explore how the simple rule of two-way interactions shows up in your relationships with children, families, and colleagues.

In your next interaction, pose a question and really listen to understand the other person's experience. Ask a follow-up question. This supports a deeper connection.

Reflecting on Relationships and Interactions

Now that you have explored the simple rules of honest, open, trusting, and two-way relationships and interactions, think about the relationships and interactions you have day to day with your family, at work, and with children you care for. As you consider the questions, think about how the simple rules can strengthen connections.

- In what ways do you share your interests and ideas with others to create more open and honest relationships and interactions?

- Do you respond to children's questions in real ways?

- How do you ensure that what you say and do helps adults and children feel secure enough to express a range of emotions in your presence?

- What clues do you look for that let you know that others trust you?

- How do you partner with the other adults in children's lives to model strong relationships and interactions for children?

Tips to Strengthen Relationships and Interactions

- Cultivate self-awareness to guide how you interact with children and adults.

- Use drop-off and pickup times as opportunities to strengthen connections between families and educators.

- Help children understand their emotions and the emotions of others by providing words and saying them out loud for children to hear and begin to understand them.

- Develop a system for exchanging information with other adults in children's lives. Examples include:

  - *Using a notebook to exchange information between families and teachers.*

  - *Having a designated place in each classroom to ensure all staff have access to information regarding the children in the class.*

  - *Establishing a text group among family members to quickly exchange or share important information.*

- *Allow time in your day for self-care. When your needs are met, you have more energy to nurture relationships and interactions.*

NOTES

Part 4

Simple Rules for the Emotional and Physical Environment

Emotional and physical environments that support everyone begin with you!

Four simple rules guide our decision making as we create spaces for young children: they are SAFE, CALM, ORGANIZED, and RESPECTFUL. Together these four rules lay the foundation for equity and respect in the emotional and physical environment.

Safe

Create safe emotional and physical environments.

Safe means protected from danger and risk. When the emotional and physical environment is safe, whether it's your home, your workplace, or a center where young children are cared for and learn, the space conveys a clear message that all are free from harm, risk, and worry. Everyone can trust that there is no threat to their physical or emotional well-being.

Secure, protected, sheltered, guarded, healthy

❖ *What words come to mind when you think about a safe emotional and physical environment?*

Luis, a teacher of three-year-olds, notices Marissa getting on a tricycle. He walks over and kneels beside her, saying, "Marissa, it's a lovely day for a tricycle ride, isn't it? I see you getting on your trike. You'd like to ride, huh? That's fabulous. Let's go grab your helmet. It's important that we keep your brain safe while you're having fun." What do you notice in this example that conveys a safe emotional and physical environment?

Understanding a Safe Emotional and Physical Environment

Consider what safe environments look like for you—both the emotional and the physical space. If you go to a park to walk and the pavement is all cracked and bumpy, you have to keep your eyes on the path to keep from falling. If children are yelled at for spilling milk while pouring, they may be more hesitant to try again. If a coworker continually dismisses your ideas, you may feel it's not safe to share them. If children are on the playground with broken equipment, they are not safe to play freely. As you read these stories, notice what safety looks like in action.

AT HOME

Cheryl is very excited. For the first time, her two-year-old grandchild, Matthew, is coming to her house for a sleepover. Cheryl makes sure she has chicken nuggets, yogurt, blueberries, peaches, Cheerios, and Goldfish, as these are some of Matthew's favorite foods. She makes sure to put breakable items out of reach. She also asks her neighbor to help install a special lock for the basement door. Beside Matthew's bed, she puts a photo of him with his two moms. She knows how important it is for Matthew to be safe and feel safe in her home. As she takes one last look around, she hears Matthew and her daughter knocking at the door.

IN A CHILDCARE SETTING

Sharma is preparing snacks for her class before the day begins. As she begins pouring the crackers into a plastic bowl so that children can scoop their own portions, she pauses to look at the box and sees it is an unfamiliar brand. She compares the ingredients on the box to the class allergy list. Noticing that soy protein is in the crackers and that one of the children can't eat soy, she decides that she will get a second choice so that everyone is safe and no one feels excluded at snack time. She will be sure to talk with Tamara, who is allergic to soy, and offer her the other type of cracker.

❖ *What did you find interesting in the examples in action?*

Think about some spaces where you've recently spent time. Did they feel safe? What made them that way?

Why Do Safe Emotional and Physical Environments Matter?

A safe environment ensures emotional and physical security for children and adults. When the emotional space is safe, everyone can express themselves without inhibition and know that others will treat them with care and respect. When we know we're safe, we are more likely to feel supported and have trust in those around us. Feeling safe in our environment allows us to focus our energies on building relationships and learning. It's not emotionally safe when we feel tense, stressed, or worried that someone will cause us harm. When the physical environment is safe, we're more comfortable and can relax. It's not safe when it is hard to breathe, too cluttered, or too hot. When we're physically uncomfortable, or in physical danger, our worry or distress interferes with our ability to do our work and relate to others.

RESEARCH TELLS US

Safe environments are the foundations for a supportive climate and culture. Clean and comfortable surroundings affect people's well-being. A climate and culture of safety communicates a powerful message of support, both within an organization and in the wider community. In businesses where workers feel psychologically safe, there is greater productivity, more internal and external collaboration, and more growth. In safe educational settings, children and adults feel emotionally supported and respected.

Safe environments encourage exploration and self-expression. Our sense of physical and emotional safety affects how we engage with our environment. In physically safe spaces, everyone, especially children, can move around freely without risk of danger. In psychologically safe spaces, adults and children are more likely to speak up, share ideas, and feel comfortable enough to ask questions. At work, this leads to stronger performance and greater productivity. A safe environment contributes to exploring new ideas, taking risks, and feeling free to make mistakes, which leads to increased confidence.

Safe environments foster positive relationships. In physically safe spaces, people relax and are more open to interactions. Our need for physical and emotional safety is linked to our ability to feel confident and be trusting in relationships. We feel safer when we're surrounded by familiar people. In environments of emotional safety, we're more likely to share our perspectives. For adults, emotionally safe environments make it easier to

build positive relationships and have authentic interactions with family, friends, and coworkers. Among children, emotionally safe environments support social and psychological development. Children explore new activities, manage challenges and transitions, and advocate for their needs.

For adults and children alike, safe environments are like welcome mats inviting us in to relax and explore. In settings for young children, a safe environment fosters trust and confidence that allows family members to leave their children, knowing that they are in good hands.

❖ *As you consider the research about safe emotional and physical environments, what feels important to you?*

Safe Emotional and Physical Environments in Communities

Notice safe emotional and physical environments shared by our partners in communities near and far.

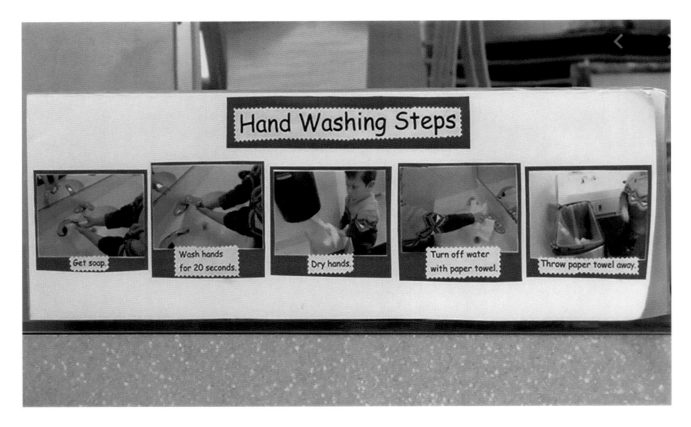

Ms. Howell encourages independence and safety for her four-year-olds by posting step-by-step handwashing instructions on a bench at the children's eye level. She uses photos of the children performing each step.

Several children in Ms. Stack's class of three-, four-, and five-year-olds have expressed fears about doctor visits and vaccines. In addition to supportive conversations and the relevant books she added to the classroom library, Ms. Stack included medical props in the dramatic play area to help children practice feeling safe. Yasmin was eager to take on the role of doctor as she experimented with taking Topher's temperature.

Shantelle values helping children understand how to respond to their emotions and the emotions of others. She and the children name emotions and discuss situations when they feel them. They talk about the strength of emotion—how big it can feel when we're sad, angry, or excited. There's a designated safe space within the classroom where a child can be when they want time alone. Shantelle reassures each child that she is always available if they want support.

❖ Invitation to Explore

Think about what it feels like to experience emotional and physical safety in an environment. What features of the environment contribute to these feelings?

What are some actions you take to create a safe space for others?

Simple Rule #6

Calm

Shape calm emotional and physical environments.

Calm means peaceful and free from disturbance. When the emotional and physical environments are calm, whether your home, office, childcare center, or outdoor recreational space, it soothes your senses. When your surroundings are calm, you can relax and easily interact, think, and learn. You're comfortable because you're free from unnecessary noise and chaos.

Soothing, comfortable, relaxed, quiet, tranquil

❖ *What words come to mind when you think about a calm emotional and physical environment?*

With a calm space arranged for her at the kitchen table so that she can work independently, Addie focuses on her exploration with watercolors, making discoveries about shapes and colors.

❖ *What do you notice in this example that conveys a calm emotional and physical environment?*

Understanding Calm Emotional and Physical Environments

What do calm spaces look like for you in the physical and emotional environment? Do fluorescent lights hurt your eyes and cause you stress? What about loud noise? What do you notice about these examples of calm emotional and physical environments?

AT HOME

Mai Lin has been operating her family childcare home for the past year. She cares for five children, ages fifteen months to thirty-six months, and has a family of her own. It's always busy, but she enjoys the children and likes that every day is different. Recently, she's noticed that she needs to make a little time for herself each day, especially as she transitions from caring for young children to caring for her own family's needs. The children are usually picked up between 4:30 and 5:00 p.m. Mai Lin has decided to take thirty minutes after the children have left each day to take a walk. After a week of adding this to her routine, she's finding it's a perfect way for her to calm her mind, relax, and be ready for her family time.

IN A CHILDCARE SETTING

Haulani recently enrolled her toddler, Caleb, at Ohai Preschool. At the end of her own workday, Haulani arrived to pick up Caleb, exhausted and eager to get home. They had a full evening of activities ahead. As she walked into the toddler room, she saw that Caleb was still asleep in his crib. Lauren, Caleb's teacher, greeted her with a warm smile, and said, "I can see from your face that you've had a long day. It took Caleb a bit longer to go down for his nap. I thought I'd give him a few extra minutes so that he would be more cheerful when you picked him up. Can you have a seat for a few minutes? We can chat and then wake him up." Haulani sat down in the rocker beside Caleb's crib, and for the first time all day, she felt her body relax from the soft chair, the quiet music, and Lauren's gentle manner. Caleb began to stir, and Lauren walked to the crib to lift him up. Caleb's smile, the few minutes of peace, and her refreshed mood helped Haulani feel ready for her evening.

❖ *What did you find interesting in the examples in action?*

Think about a space where you've recently spent time. Was it calm? How did the calm environment support you? What made it calm?

Why Do Calm Emotional and Physical Environments Matter?

A calm emotional and physical environment is a peaceful and secure setting that opens the door for relationships and learning. The light, sounds, colors, and textures of the physical space can soothe the senses, which in turn contribute to a relaxed emotional atmosphere. Calm environments support feelings of safety and security, creating opportunities for communication, exploration, and growth without fear of disruption or distraction. Calmness in the environment supports self-regulation and resiliency. It sends the message that you can relax, explore, and think.

RESEARCH TELLS US

Calm environments keep us mindful. A calm emotional and physical environment offers predictability and stability, and encourages us to be in the present moment. When children and adults are surrounded by order and harmony, it's easier to keep our emotions balanced and to act with intention. Being outdoors in a calm, natural environment supports engagement, motivation to learn, and cooperative interactions.

Calm environments help us build stronger relationships. Being calm is important for adults and children. When the physical environment is hectic, noisy, or cluttered, it works against feeling calm. It can create stress and tension that undermine positive interactions. On the other hand, when we feel calm and relaxed, we are more open to trusting others. When we're calm, we're more likely to be genuine and authentic. Calm settings for children lead to deeper engagement and interactions with peers. When workplace supervisors create calm environments, employees are more effective and more likely to work collaboratively.

Calm environments support more resilient communities. Even when we experience calm in one environment, chaos in another can disrupt our sense of internal balance. Among children, unpredictable home environments raise stress hormone levels. When children can engage in predictable routines, they are more likely to be active in their communities. This points to the importance of fostering calm across all our environments, so that we can move from place to place and know that we'll find consistency.

Calm environments invite us to relax and consider possibilities for interactions and learning. We want to come back to such spaces again and again.

❖ *As you consider the research about calm emotional and physical environments, what feels important to you?*

Calm Emotional and Physical Environments in Communities

Notice some of the features in these emotional and physical environments shared by our partners that make them calm.

The owner and director of this childcare center knows how important it is for her staff to have a quiet place to decompress during breaks. She has set up a small office for staff members so they have a space separate from the busyness of their day to make a phone call, use the computer, or just sit and think.

Marvin loves the public library, and he and his older brother spend at least one afternoon weekly there. Marvin gets lost in the books and always wants a private, quiet spot to read. Rakia, the librarian, knows that finding his perfect spot to read is important to Marvin. She enjoys watching to see how he creates a calm setting for this special time.

With some help from Mom, Tae has found a calm, quiet space to spend time alone with his tablet.

❖ Invitation to Explore

What features of the emotional and physical environment help you feel calm?

When someone walks into a space that you create, at home or at work, what feelings do you think they experience?

Organized

Design organized emotional and physical environments.

Organized means having an intentional plan or structure. When the emotional and physical environments are organized, whether at home, at work, or in a setting for young children's care and learning, careful planning supports everyone's well-being and effectiveness. An organized physical environment means that everything has a place that is clear and intentional. When we think about an organized environment, we also consider the predictability of the schedule, because this contributes to our sense of well-being.

Systematic, methodical, orderly, accessible, uncluttered

❖ *What words come to mind when you think about an organized emotional and physical environment?*

93

A new parent walks into Garden Early Learning to register her child for care. Liz, the receptionist, says, "Good morning, I'm Liz. How can I help you?" The new parent says, "Hi, my name is Rachel Santiago, and I'd like to register my child, Pia, for care." Liz invites Rachel over to some comfortable chairs in the office and says, "Tell me about your child, Ms. Santiago." Rachel immediately feels comfortable with Liz and settles in to chat.

❖ *What do you notice in this example that conveys an organized emotional and physical environment?*

Understanding Organized Emotional and Physical Environments

Consider what an organized emotional and physical environment can look like in different settings.

AT HOME

Evette has been in the position of executive director at her town's community recreation center for four months. It's so hectic that she feels more like a firefighter than the ED, and most days she stays late to catch up on unfinished tasks. Feeling overwhelmed, she decides to get organized. She takes thirty minutes to tidy up her office and decides to try two new techniques. At the end of each day, she clears her desk and creates a to-do list for the next day. She also closes her office door for one hour each day and posts a sign that reads: Brain Work: Please do not disturb. Evette notices that after a few days, she feels less stress, is accomplishing more, and has time to check in with her colleagues.

IN A CHILDCARE SETTING

Paul is a teacher of three-year-olds. As he prepares to welcome the children back from winter break, he remembers the importance of organization in the classroom. When children enter, they know what to do, where to go, and how to get what they need. He's made one change in the room: switching the block and art areas for easier access to water for cleanup. He's curious to see how the children will respond. On this first day back, Nathan comes to Paul and says, "What happened to the blocks?" Paul invites him to keep looking around the room to see if he can spot the block area. Another child says, "Hey, the art area moved too." In the morning meeting, the class thinks together about the reasons for the changes and how the new arrangement will help them with their work.

❖ *What did you find interesting in the examples in action?*

Think about some spaces where you've recently spent time. Were they organized? What made them organized? How did the organization make you feel?

❖ *As you consider the research about organized emotional and physical environments, what feels important to you?*

Why Do Organized Emotional and Physical Environments Matter?

When the emotional and physical environment is organized, it conveys the message "I have what I need to be effective." When spaces are free from clutter and accessible to all, it's easier to make effective decisions and be independent. Organization fosters self-regulation—the ability to manage our behavior and reactions. Organization creates an emotional climate where adults and children can make decisions and be independent. Organized emotional and physical environments make learning, relationships, and communication easier.

RESEARCH TELLS US

Organized environments make us more productive. Research shows that being in organized spaces positively affects productivity, learning outcomes, stress levels, and independence. For children, organized classrooms support learning, well-being, confidence, and social interactions. Planning and intention are key to creating organized spaces. When teachers spend more time at the beginning of the school year supporting children in creating and understanding the rules, procedures, and routines of classroom life, everyone can focus more on interactions and learning throughout the year.

Organized environments encourage balanced emotions. Being organized in our environment helps us get along better with others, personally and professionally. Organized environments at work increase employee satisfaction and decrease workplace bullying. At home, organized household routines support everyone's emotional regulation, which is very beneficial to children. When children's environments are organized and predictable, they are less likely to become upset, angry, or defiant.

Organized environments invite collaboration. Organized spaces allow us to think more clearly, communicate more effectively, and learn more easily than disorganized spaces. Organized environments have also been shown to minimize conflict and lead to more productive and satisfied community members.

Organized emotional and physical environments are critical for adults and children alike. Organization invites our subconscious to be at ease. When we know where things are and what we can expect, we can focus on what we want to accomplish, whether we are four or forty.

Organized Emotional and Physical Environments in Communities

Notice organized emotional and physical environments shared by our partners in communities near and far.

This outdoor space for young children is intentionally planned to encourage exploration and collaboration. While space is defined and several structures fixed, there is ample opportunity for open-ended play and flexible thinking.

Four-year-old Rory learns about independence, responsibility, and organization as he assists with setting up for lunch.

At Gabriel's mixed-income program, the staff members are committed to making sure all families feel included. Ample clean clothes are a privilege they do not expect every family to have. These boxes, labeled according to size, ensure there are always extra clothes of all sizes so teachers can easily find what they need if there is an accident or a joyful day in a mud puddle.

❖ Invitation to Explore

What happens for you when you are in an organized space?

How do you think that relates to an organized environment for children?

Simple Rule #8

Respectful

Promote respectful emotional and physical environments.

Respectful means showing regard and consideration for someone or something. When the emotional and physical environment is respectful—at home, at work, or in a child-care setting—the message conveyed when you enter the space is "You belong here." Your values and needs are welcomed and appreciated.

Considerate, accommodating, kind, fair, responsive

❖ *What words come to mind when you think about respectful emotional and physical environments?*

Monica, a teacher of infants, is changing the diaper of ten-month-old Amari. As she talks with Amari, Lee, an eight-month-old, wakes up, stands, and begins to babble for Monica's attention. Monica says, "Amari, Lee is awake. I'm going to talk to him while I change your diaper so he knows that we're right here. "Hi, Lee. We hear you, honey. I'm changing Amari and will come to get you as soon as I'm done. Let's all sing together." She begins to sing "Hello Sunshine," a song Lee's mom has taught Monica to soothe Lee. He begins to coo. What do you notice in this example that conveys a respectful emotional and physical environment?

Understanding Respectful Emotional and Physical Environments

Consider what respectful environments look like for you. Imagine you go to a conference with a teacher and have to sit in a child-size chair. Or you enter a store or restaurant, and the music is so loud it is impossible to hear. A respectful environment considers your physical and emotional needs. As you read these stories, notice what respectful emotional and physical environments look like in action.

AT HOME

Three-year-old Kara likes to choose her clothes each day. The problem is that her clothing is folded in drawers, and it's too hard for Kara to reach inside, see what's there, make her choice, and keep things in order. Kara's mom, Ami, gets frustrated by the mess but realizes that it's important for Kara to be independent. Together, they sort Kara's shirts, pants, underwear, and socks in open baskets on the floor along the end of Kara's bed. Rather than folding, which is too hard for Kara, they practice making "roll-ups," which Kara calls sausages. The redesign shows Ami's respect for Kara's needs. It's a win-win: Kara is delighted and Ami feels less stress.

IN A CHILDCARE SETTING

Bituin, a teacher at Little Kids Academy, believes birthdays are special and should be celebrated. When she was a little girl in the Philippines, her birthday was celebrated at home and at school. However, she is beginning to wonder if her love of birthdays is respectful to all families in the program. While some families bring treats, others are either unable or choose not to. Bituin decides to bring this to a staff meeting to discuss with her colleagues. They decide that to be respectful and to honor their community's diversity, they will invite each family to choose a special book to be read to the class on the child's birthday or on a day that the family chooses.

❖ *What did you notice about the stories of respectful emotional and physical environments?*
Think about spaces you've been in that have felt respectful. What made them respectful?

Why Do Respectful Emotional and Physical Environments Matter?

When emotional and physical environments are respectful, everyone feels that they are welcome and they belong. The physical space reflects a diversity of values and needs. We know that others are listening to us, acknowledging our points of view, and making any needed adjustments. We, in turn, extend the same respect to others. This is clear from research, which shows that respectful emotional and physical environments create a sense of safety and support.

RESEARCH TELLS US

Respectful environments foster a sense of belonging. When we feel that we belong, those around us reinforce that we are valued contributors to our environments. In early learning programs, families and children are more likely to thrive when they feel seen and heard in the center or program. In workplaces with cultures of respect, employees feel more engaged with their work, more resilient in overcoming challenges, and more satisfied with their jobs. Receiving messages of respect from managers and colleagues makes employees more likely to stay with an organization.

Respectful environments are safe for all voices. In respectful environments, adults and children alike are more likely to speak openly and have two-way relationships. We feel that we can share our thoughts, and others feel safe to share with us. In our working relationships, when we feel that we can respectfully share our thoughts, we can respond to challenges in a more collaborative way. Environments of respect are especially important when dealing with diverse perspectives, conflict, and disagreement.

Respectful environments encourage shared understanding. In cultures of respect, we're listening and learning from each other, treating everyone's contributions as equally important. Safe and empathetic environments for teachers, families, and children, for example, help ensure that all adults are working with a shared vision to support children's social and emotional development. Respect spreads across an environment, interaction by interaction. At school, teachers who model respect for their students also gain respect from their students, and students are more likely to have respectful relationships with their peers.

For both children and adults, respectful emotional and physical environments are key to creating and reinforcing cultures of well-being. They remind us that, no matter where we go, everyone deserves space that enables them to engage as their full selves.

❖ *As you consider the research about respectful emotional and physical environments, what feels important to you?*

Respectful Emotional and Physical Environments in Communities

Notice respectful emotional and physical environments shared by our partners in communities near and far.

The educators in this early-learning program have created an outdoor classroom where the arrangement of space and the materials invites respect for nature and children's curiosity.

Gretchen, a teacher of three-, four-, and five-year-olds, respectfully invites them to contribute to the display of artwork in the classroom. One child worked on the sign explaining what the display is about. Children were asked to choose a collage to contribute to the display, and a few children asked to have their photo included.

In this classroom, children demonstrate respect for the environment by collecting everyday recyclable items and learning as they stack, sort, count, and describe their attributes. Experiences such as these are respectful of children's joy in using open-ended materials with flexibility and inventiveness.

❖ Invitation to Explore

What features of the emotional and physical environment make it feel respectful for you?

How does that relate to a respectful environment for children?

Reflecting on the Emotional and Physical Environment

We've explored the simple rules for the emotional and physical environments: they are safe, calm, organized, and respectful. Think about the spaces you are in with members of your family, at work, and with children you care for. As you consider the questions, think about how the simple rules of safe, calm, organized, and respectful can help to create thriving communities, at home, at work, and for children.

- In all the different settings of home, work, and childcare, how do you ensure children and families know what to expect in the environment? How is it organized so that it is predictable and respectful?

- Take a moment to look around the environment. Can families see themselves reflected respectfully in this space?

- Does the environment support independence and self-regulation for adults and children? Does it reflect the belief that children are competent and capable learners?

- Is the environment safe and calm so that it is possible to focus and be productive?

- Does the environment ensure children's rights are being preserved in daily activities?

Tips to Create Emotional and Physical Environments That Support Everyone

- Get to know people's names and use them for greetings and in conversation.

- In childcare settings, invite families to share foods, artifacts, or other things that show they are fully welcome in the space.

- Use soft colors to support a calm environment and promote self-regulation for children and adults.

- When choosing furniture, consider the age and abilities of the children and adults who will be using the space.

- In childcare settings, use your policies and procedures to ensure families and staff know what to expect in the environment.

NOTES

Part 5

Simple Rules for Learning Experiences

Optimal learning experiences begin with you!

Three simple rules guide our decision making as we create learning experiences for young children: they are MEANINGFUL, EXPLORATORY, and ACTIONABLE. Together these three rules lay the foundation for learning experiences that demonstrate equity and respect.

Meaningful

Plan meaningful learning experiences.

Meaningful is defined as relevant and significant. When learning experiences are meaningful, they connect to the learner's interests and are important to the learner. The knowledge, skills, or concepts that you are learning make sense to you because you can connect this new information to knowledge and experience you already have. This is true for children and adults.

Relevant, familiar, worthwhile, purposeful, significant

❖ *What words, phrases, or personal stories come to mind when you think about meaningful learning experiences for you and for children?*

117

Caitlyn has children of different ages in her family childcare home. The children spontaneously decided they wanted to know the length of the living room. Their interest and curiosity sparked the mathematical challenge, and Caitlyn provided some tools. Together the children collaborated to figure out the answer.

Understanding Meaningful Learning Experiences

Consider these examples of meaningful learning.

IN THE WORKPLACE

At a Head Start Center, teachers and assistant teachers recognize that when they get along well with each other, and relationships are harmonious, there are fewer challenging behaviors with children. Two teachers suggested that they use a staff meeting to identify the challenges of working in partnership with another adult; one a person you know, and one you don't. They formed teams and identified a strategy they could try. Because this is a problem they grapple with each day, they are ready and eager to learn and test new ideas. By choosing a learning strategy to address a relevant situation, everyone was engaged, and they generated many new ideas for improving classroom partnerships.

IN A CHILDCARE SETTING

Joel is a teacher in a classroom for two-year-olds. In the spring, he sees how independent the children have become and wants to give them a more active role in putting away their sheets and blankets after naptime. First, he explains to them that each day he puts their sheets and blankets away carefully, so they stay clean and are easy to find. He lets them know they are ready to do this important job. Next, he demonstrates how to fold and store their items. For the next several days he provides close support and sings a cleanup song as children put away their sheets and blankets. The children are proud of their accomplishments, and several show their parents at pickup time. After weeks of the new routine, the children are independently storing their sheets and blankets. By intentionally responding to the children's desire for independence and introducing the new responsibility in a way children could understand, cleanup after naptime is now relaxed and efficient.

❖ *As you read the examples of meaningful learning experiences, what made them meaningful in your eyes?*

Think about a recent learning experience. Did it feel meaningful to you? If so, why? If not, why not?

Why Do Meaningful Learning Experiences Matter?

When children and adults have meaningful learning experiences, they establish connections between new information and what they already know. This connection validates why the new information is important and makes it easier to remember and apply. Research supports the importance of meaningful learning experiences, showing us how they encourage confidence, independence, and connection with others.

RESEARCH TELLS US

Meaningful learning experiences connect to our everyday reality. We care about what touches us. When we can find a personal, emotional connection to what we're learning, it usually sticks. While people might recall a set of facts for a test in the short term, we're more likely to retain new information when it connects to lived experience. When a child who loves pizza visits a pizza store and observes how the pizza is made, that child is likely to remember many details and facts about the equipment used, each worker's specific job, and the process of making the pizza.

Meaningful learning experiences show why new information is important. When we can see the personal importance of what we're learning, we're more likely to hold on to it and use it as the basis for learning more. When we feel confident about applying new information, we are more open to sharing our knowledge and helping others see its importance.

Meaningful learning experiences connect to our social world. Learning is often a social experience. Connections with others can make learning experiences meaningful. This is true for children and adults. When children sense excitement from adults about a topic, they are often likely to join in the learning.

Adults and children alike need meaningful learning experiences! By communicating how new information is relevant and important, we foster a sense of agency and joy in learning.

❖ *As you consider the research about meaningful learning experiences, what feels important to you?*

Meaningful Learning Experiences in Communities

Observe meaningful learning experiences in communities near and far.

Grandad arrived early for Thanksgiving dinner and was surprised to see Weston rolling the lumpia (Filipino spring rolls). He joined him at the table as Weston showed him the lumpia rolling techniques he's been working on since he was two.

Randall and his daughters decide they want to plant herbs. They are all excited about doing the project together. Reusing old drink containers as plant pots, they enjoy checking each day to see how the plants are progressing.

Saba and her family have just moved into a new neighborhood. She and her daughter, Pari, frequently took walks where they lived before, noticing different features of the environment. To familiarize Pari and her baby brother with their new surroundings, she takes them for an afternoon stroll, inviting lots of conversation about what they see and hear around them.

❖ Invitation to Explore

What makes learning meaningful for you?

What helps you to create meaningful learning experiences for children or adults?

Simple Rule #10

Exploratory

Introduce exploratory learning experiences.

Exploratory means investigative and experimental. Exploratory learning experiences allow for probing, fact-finding, and analysis. For children and adults, exploratory learning experiences allow the learner to experiment, handle materials, and use trial and error to find out what happens when you do this or that.

Investigative, open-ended, probing, searching

❖ *What words, phrases, or personal stories come to mind when you think about exploratory learning experiences?*

127

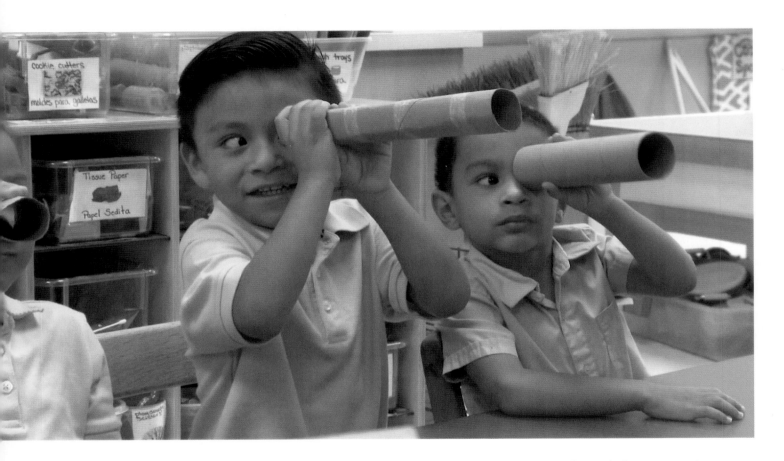

After inviting families to send recycled paper towel and toilet paper rolls to the classroom, the children are experimenting with the cylinders.

Understanding Exploratory Learning Experiences

Consider these examples of exploratory learning.

AT HOME

Katarina and her partner, Roselle, want to try camping with their two children, ages four and ten. Katarina loved camping as a child, but it's different being the responsible adult. Where would they go? How could they get camping equipment without spending a lot of money? And what about bears? Katarina begins to write her questions down in a notebook. She involves the rest of the family in asking questions and finding answers, jotting ideas in what they call their adventure notebook. The children are eager to see animals and go swimming. Katarina finds friends who offer to lend them gear, and the family reads about how to be "bear aware." They choose a campsite with a lake and lots of wildlife. The whole family is bubbling with excitement.

IN A CHILDCARE SETTING

Yesenia, a teacher of three- and four-year-olds, knows that children enjoy mixing colors. Today, she notices that Jayquon is adding white paint to one of her carefully prepared primary color paint cups. Quelling her urge to correct, she observes as he squirts it in and uses the brush to paint a stripe of this new color next to a line of red. Yesenia kneels beside him and says, "Oh my goodness, I'm seeing you found a new way to make colors! You put white paint in the red paint! I wonder what will happen?" Jayquon says, "Look, white and red!" and points to a stroke of unmixed paint on the paper. Yesenia says "Hmm, it looks like the red and white are separate." Jayquon puts his brush in the paint cup and swirls the paint together, then makes another stroke. Yesenia says, "Oh, the color changed! Now it's pink! Jayquon, you put red and white together and made pink!"

❖ *What did you find interesting in the examples in action?*

    Think about a recent learning experience you had. Was it exploratory? What made it that way?

Why Do Exploratory Learning Experiences Matter?

When learning experiences are exploratory, we get messy! There's hands-on investigation and research. We are masters of our own questions, discovering the answers through trial and error. Research shows that learning experiences emphasizing exploration increase the buy-in or ownership and allow us to remain open to learning independently and from others.

RESEARCH TELLS US

Exploratory learning experiences are opportunities to set our own learning paths. For adults and children, learning through exploration lets us use all our physical senses to understand our environment and our experiences. We follow what catches our attention as a path to deeper understanding. When teachers encourage children to experiment, inside and outside the classroom, children learn how they can use their skills and abilities to make discoveries about their environment.

Exploratory learning experiences keep us open to new ideas. Open exploration leads to more innovative thinking. Learners who are encouraged to explore new ideas are better able to cope with uncertainty and to persist in seeking solutions.

Exploratory learning experiences encourage us to learn with and from others. As we explore, we often find others with similar interests. We might come upon opportunities to share our new learning with those around us. For preschool-age children, exploring new and unfamiliar objects not only leads to deeper understanding, it also increases their confidence in talking about their experiences with other children and adults.

For both adults and children, exploratory learning experiences open up new ways to engage with the world around us and reinforce our sense of agency. They keep us thinking creatively and seeking innovation and discovery.

❖ *As you consider the research about exploratory learning experiences, what feels important to you?*

Exploratory Learning Experiences in Communities

Observe exploratory learning experiences in communities near and far.

At Tory's family childcare program in Wyoming, very young children can safely experiment as carpenters, using tools and wood.

Margot, the teacher of these preschoolers, combines cornstarch and water to make "goop" and puts it in the water table so that children can use language and their senses to explore texture, thickness, and motion.

Family members are invited to the classroom to explore how they can support their children's acquisition of math and literacy skills using natural materials from the environment.

❖ Invitation to Explore

Think about a recent learning experience you enjoyed. In what ways was it exploratory?

Think about a recent learning experience you shared with a child. How did you explore? How did the child explore? What was your interaction like?

Simple Rule #11

◆

Actionable

Devise actionable learning experiences.

Actionable means practical and useful. When learning is actionable, you can put it into practice for different purposes. When we learn something new, we come to own this new knowledge by applying it. Actionable learning experiences invite the learner to actively construct knowledge in ways that help them experience success, conveying the message "You are smart and capable." This applies to learning for children and adults.

Useful, practical, purposeful, usable, functional

❖ *What words, phrases, or personal stories come to mind when you think of actionable learning experiences?*

Serenity was eager to learn how to string beads to make jewelry. She and Danielle, her mom, ordered a bunch of multicolored beads, nylon thread, and clasps online. Together they are learning how to use the beads to make jewelry, and Serenity can't wait to wear what she makes.

Understanding Actionable Learning Experiences

Consider these examples of actionable learning.

AT HOME

Four-year-old Josie is disappointed she can't wear her favorite "Bug Expert" shirt to preschool because it's in the laundry. Eric, her dad, says, "Tomorrow is Saturday, a home day. How about if you help me wash the laundry?" The following morning, Josie reminds her dad about washing her shirt. Eric shows Josie how to gather the laundry from around the apartment, getting the towels from the bathroom and the clothes from her little sister's room. Eric helps her pick out dark-colored clothing, like Josie's shirt, that will go in the wash together. They make a load that includes the bug shirt, and Josie puts it in the washer. She asks her dad to help with detergent and shuts the door. Josie is now a laundry expert!

IN A CHILDCARE SETTING

Election Day was approaching, and some of the older children at Global Connections Learning Center were talking about which candidate they wanted to vote for. Other children had lots of questions. What is voting? Doesn't running mean moving fast? Several teachers decided that this was a great teaching and learning opportunity. During the week prior to Election Day, they built voting booths, created ballots, and sent information home to families. The children viewed pictures of the candidates for president and shared their knowledge of the candidates. On Election Day, parents assisted their children in voting. Children and families moved through the steps of the voting process—making a choice, marking it down, and submitting it to be counted. Each child received an "I VOTED!" sticker.

❖ *What did you find interesting in the examples you just read?*

Think about a recent learning experience you had. Was it actionable? What made it that way?

Why Do Actionable Learning Experiences Matter?

Actionable learning experiences allow us to apply new skills or knowledge to our everyday activities. We learn by doing, engaging with others and the environment. Brazilian teacher Paulo Freire first pioneered modern ideas about actionable learning in the 1960s and 1970s. He rejected the idea that the learner is an "empty vessel" to be filled with knowledge. Instead, Freire said, good teachers and good education systems see learners as cocreators of knowledge. Generations of educators have been inspired by Freire's work to engage learners in actionable experiences. Research shows that actionable learning has been proven to support deeper, more meaningful, and long-lasting learning.

RESEARCH TELLS US

Actionable learning experiences build confidence. In some environments, learning is synonymous with reading, memorizing, and listening to lessons. Actionable learning creates opportunities to practice and apply new information. The learners gain confidence as they discover uses for what is learned, and they have a greater sense of ownership over their new knowledge.

Actionable learning experiences encourage creative problem solving. Hands-on learning reinforces why information matters in context. It gives a real-world view into challenges and possible solutions. When learning is actionable, it leads to further questions. Actionable learning experiences spark curiosity.

Actionable learning experiences generate collaboration. When children and adults engage in actionable learning, there are more questions to ask and many perspectives to consider. Learning with others requires actively listening and exchanging information. This leads to creative, flexible, and successful strategies to solve problems.

When learning experiences are actionable, we can incorporate new information and ideas into our day to day. Through our actionable learning experiences, we make an impact on the world around us as we learn.

❖ *As you consider the research about actionable learning experiences, what feels important to you?*

Actionable Learning Experiences in Communities

Observe actionable learning experiences in communities near and far.

Good night, little kitten
Lay down your sleep

Notice how this little one is reading a bedtime story. While her parents sit close beside her and gently prop the book for support, a fledgling reader is learning how to look at the pictures, hold the book, and turn the pages to see what happens next in the story.

Gracie is making waffles and she's a confident learner. She selects and measures the ingredients by reading the recipe and stirs the batter to just the right consistency.

Diego and his aunt, Renata, are outside planting beans in Renata's yard. Diego is practicing how to use the nozzle to get just the right flow of water.

❖ *What do you notice in these examples?*

❖ Invitation to Explore

What happens for you when your learning experiences are actionable?
Can you think of a recent one?

We invite you to notice how your decisions create actionable learning experiences
for children and adults.

Reflecting on Learning Experiences

You have been reading about the simple rules for learning experiences—they are meaningful, exploratory, and actionable. Think about experiences you have at home and at work where your curiosity is sparked, you are asking questions and extending your learning. How does this show up for you? How do you learn with colleagues? With members of your family? With children? As you consider the questions, think about how the simple rules of meaningful, exploratory, and actionable learning can support thriving communities, at home, at work, and for children.

- Think of a recent learning experience you had with your family. Was everyone interested? In what ways did it nurture curiosity?

- As you plan meetings for adults, how can you invite conversations that draw out the wisdom and experiences of the group?

- When you are with more than one child, how do you support their individual and collective interests?

- How do you connect learning opportunities to children's interests and questions?

- What are some ways you invite children to use materials in the environment in various ways?

Tips for Creating Optimal Learning Experiences

- Allow ample time for children to explore and engage with materials and follow their curiosity.

- Demonstrate respect for learners. For example, invite children to label their materials if they aren't finished with them. With adults, allow ample time for discussions and conversations in meetings.

- Plan for new possibilities when creating an agenda or lesson plan. Flexibility and surprises make learning more interesting.

- Invite children and adults to think about how they will use new information.

- Invite conversation and exchange of ideas to encourage learning with and from others.

NOTES

Part 6

Taking Action

In the opening of the book, we invited you to consider how humanity—being kind, having empathy, and treating people with dignity and respect—begins with each one of us. We must embrace our role as leaders for children. We have seen that communities who decide to practice the 11 Simple Rules together make progress on the path to more equitable, thriving communities for children and for ourselves. With effective relationships and interactions, a healthy emotional and physical environment, and engaging learning experiences, we can powerfully affect young children's learning, their emotional well-being, even their physical health, today and in the future. All children deserve to thrive, and we believe that together, we can make sure they do.

Yes, it's hard to consistently be an in-tune, responsive, encouraging partner with children and other adults. Of course, some days are tiring and others overwhelming. But we can resist the fight-or-flight instinct that comes with stress, and instead tap into our willingness to be leaders. We can support each other by having more productive interactions. We can empower ourselves to act intentionally even in difficult circumstances. These capacities are broadly known as executive functioning, the brain-based abilities to be clear about our intentions, stay focused on them even when distracted, and adjust when needed. When we are clear about our goals, self-aware enough to be proactive instead of reactive, and able to sustain our actions over time, we can stay true to our intentions. Over time we even literally rewire our brains so that we engage in a positive cycle of growth.

It is our hope that the 11 Simple Rules will support you in being who you hope to be for each other and for children, no matter the circumstances. And as we sustain these practices over time, we can consistently think and act in the ways we know lead to more equitable, thriving communities.

How You Can Begin

START WITH SELF.

If there's one thing I've learned in life, it's the power of using your voice. —Michelle Obama

Too often, we wait for "someday" when things will change. In truth, the power is within us to effect change. We invite you to begin by owning your sense of agency. When we understand that we have an impact on the world around us, we become more intentional in making decisions that guide our words and actions.

Have inclusive conversations. At Leading for Children, we bring people within communities together to form Learning Networks. These people represent many diverse roles in a child's ecosystem. We see how thriving communities take shape—how members from diverse backgrounds develop shared language, welcome others into learning conversations, and cocreate coherent visions of equity and quality.

Create welcoming dialogue using the 11 Simple Rules as a starting point. People need to be comfortable with each other in order to break down communication barriers within the community. In this way everyone feels safe to take part and share. We suggest you use the questions, reflections, and photos throughout the book to ignite conversation. Begin to take pictures in your own communities and use them for conversation.

A colleague in California said, "Dreams are important. When we're in community and we share our dreams, they can be actualized. What are our shared dreams?"

As adults within the child's ecosystem, we are models, advocates, champions, caregivers, curiosity sparkers, play and thought partners. To create the world our children deserve, each one of us must learn to share values, vision, and a sense of belonging. We must call upon our humanity to see the dignity, beauty, worth, and unique qualities of each person and every community. This means coming together in ways that are respectful, equitable, and accessible to all. While the 11 Simple Rules are not the single answer, we've learned that they are a necessary step to getting there. Our Learning Networks are providing the collaborative learning experiences that bring us closer to an ecosystem where all children and adults can thrive. We invite you to join us!

References

Part 1: Welcome

Lombardi, J. "To Thrive: A Goal for Children Everywhere." *Early Childhood Matters* (2019). https://earlychildhoodmatters.online/2019/to-thrive-a-goal-for-children-everywhere/.

Part 2: The 11 Simple Rules Framework

Center on the Developing Child. *The Science of Early Childhood Development* (2007). Retrieved from www.developingchild.harvard.edu.

Part 3: Simple Rules for Relationships and Interactions

General

Cekaite, A., and M. Andrén. "Children's Laughter and Motion Sharing with Peers and Adults in Preschool." *Frontiers in Psychology* 10, no. 852 (2019): 1–19.

Center for the Study of Social Policy. "Strengthening Families: A Protective Factors Framework." Washington, D.C.: Center for the Study of Social Policy.

Hyde, R., and B. Weathington. "The Congruence of Personal Values and Work Attitudes." *Genetic, Social and General Psychology Monographs* 132, no. 2 (2006): 151–90.

Simon, P., and N. Nader-Grosbois. 2021. "Preschoolers' Empathy Profiles and Their Social Adjustment." *Frontiers in Psychology* 12 (2021): 1–16.

Honest

Dammann, O. et al. "The Essence of Authenticity." *Frontiers in Psychology* 11 (2021): 1–6.

Gouveia, T., M. Shulz, and M. E. Costa. "Authenticity in Relationships: Predicting Caregiving and Attachment in Adult Romantic Relationships." *Journal of Counseling Psychology* 63, no. 6 (2016): 736–44.

Hays, C., and L. J. Carver. "Follow the Liar: The Effects of Adult Lies on Children's Honesty. *Developmental Science* 17, no. 6 (2014): 977–83.

He, T. S., and L. Qin. "On the Developmental Origin of Intrinsic Honesty." *PLOS One* 15, no. 9 (2020). Retrieved from https://journals.plos.org/plosone/article?id=10.1371/journal.pone.0238241.

Sweetland, S. "Authenticity and Sense of Power in Enabling School Structures: An Empirical Analysis." *Journal of Educational Administration* 42, no. 4 (2001)): 462–78.

Talwar, V., S. Tachison, and K. Leduc. "Promoting Honesty: The Influence of Stories on Children's Lie-Telling Behaviours and Moral Understanding." *Infant and Child Development* 25 (2016): 484–501.

Open

Alteren, G., and A. A. Tudoran. "Open-Mindedness and Adaptive Business Style: Competencies That Contribute to Building Relationships in Dissimilar Export Markets." *International Marketing Review* 36, no. 3 (2019): 365–90.

Fuertes, M., et al. "How Different Are Parents and Educators? A Comparative Study of Interactive Differences Between Parents and Educators in a Collaborative Adult-Child Activity. *PLOS One* 13, no. 11 (2018), e0205991: 1–15.

Koay, W. I., and D. Dillon. "Community Gardening: Stress, Well-Being, and Resilience Potentials." *International Journal of Environmental Research and Public Health*, 17, no. 18 (2020): 6740.

Kochanska, G., et al. "Parents' Personality and Infants' Temperament as Contributors to Their Emerging Relationships." *Journal of Personality and Social Psychology* 86, no. 5 (2004): 744–59.

Kwong, J. M. C. "Open-Mindedness as Engagement." *Southern Journal of Philosophy* 54, no. 1 (2016): 70–86.

Lord, M. "Group Learning Capacity: The Roles of Open-Mindedness and Shared Vision." *Frontiers in Psychology* 6, no. 150 (2015): 1–11.

Trusting

Kramer, R. M. "Trust and Distrust in Organizations: Emerging Perspectives, Enduring Questions." *Annual Review of Psychology* 50 (1999): 569–98.

Kudesia, R. S., and C. S. Reina. "Does Interacting with Trustworthy People Enhance Mindfulness? An Experience Sampling Study of Mindfulness in Everyday Situations." *PLOS One* 14, no. 4 (2019), e0215810. Retrieved from https://pubmed.ncbi.nlm.nih.gov/31026302/.

Van Maele, D., and M. Van Houtte. "The Quality of School Life: Teacher-Student Trust Relationships and the Organizational School Context. *Social Indicators Research* 100, no. 1 (2011): 85–100.

Mazutis, D., and N. Slawinski. "Leading Organizational Learning Through Authentic Dialogue." *Management Learning* 39, no. 4 (2008): 437–56.

Two-Way

Alsarve, J. "Friendship, Reciprocity and Similarity: Lone Mothers and Their Relationships with Friends." *Community, Work, and Family* 23, no. 4 (2020): 401–18.

Devi, V. R. "Employee Engagement Is a Two-Way Street." *Human Resource Management International Digest* 17, no. 2 (2009): 3–4.

Lindsey, E. W., et al. "Mother–Child and Father–Child Mutuality in Two Contexts: Consequences for Young Children's Peer Relationships." *Infant and Child Development* 19 (2010): 142–60.

Vaquera, E., and G. Kao. "Do You Like Me as Much as I Like You? Friendship Reciprocity and Its Effects on School Outcomes Among Adolescents." *Social Science Research* 37 (2008): 55–72.

Volmer, J., et al. "Reciprocal Relationships Between Leader–Member Exchange (LMX) and Job Satisfaction: A Cross-Lagged Analysis." *Applied Psychology* 60, no. 4 (2011): 522–45.

Part 4: Simple Rules for Emotional and Physical Environment

General

Ata, S., A. Deniz, and B. Akman. "The Physical Environment Factors in Preschools in Terms of Environmental Psychology: A Review." *Procedia: Social and Behavioral Sciences* 46 (2012): 2034–39.

Foraster, M., et al. "Exposure to Road Traffic Noise and Cognitive Development in Schoolchildren in Barcelona, Spain: A Population-Based Cohort Study." *PLOS Med* 19, no. 6 (2022), e1004001. https://doi.org/10.1371/journal.pmed.1004001.

Kahkashan, A., and V. Shivakumar. 2015. "Effects of Traffic Noise Around Schools on Attention and Memory in Primary School Children." *International Journal of Clinical and Experimental Physiology* 2, no. 3 (2015): 176–79. https://www.ijcep.org/index.php/ijcep/article/view/94.

Loebach, J., et al. "Paving the Way for Outdoor Play: Examining Socio-Environmental Barriers to Community-Based Outdoor Play." *International Journal of Environmental Research and Public Health* 18, no. 3617 (2021): 1–25.

Seiler, C. W., et al. "Long-Term Promotive and Protective Effects of Early Childcare Quality on the Social-Emotional Development in Children." *Frontiers In Psychology* 13 (2022): 1–15.

Safe

Edmondson, A. C., and L. Zhike. "Psychological Safety: The History, Renaissance, and Future of an Interpersonal Construct." *Annual Review of Organizational Psychology and Organizational Behavior* 1 (2014): 23–43.

Meheux, M. 2009. "What Makes Children Feel Safe in School? An Evaluation of the Preventative Model for Behaviour in a Local Authority with a Focus on Children's and Adults' Perspectives of Safety." Doctoral dissertation, University of London, 2009.

Moore, T., and M. McArthur. "You Feel It in Your Body: How Australian Children and Young People Think About and Experience Feeling and Being Safe." *Children & Society* 31 (2017): 206–81.

Robinson, L., et al. "Conceptualizing and Measuring Safe, Stable, Nurturing Relationships and Environmentsi Educational Settings." *Journal of Child and Family Studies* 25, no. 5 (2016): 1488–1504.

Wanless, S. B. "The Role of Psychological Safety in Human Development." *Research in Human Development* 13, no. 1 (2016): 6–14.

Calm

Brown, E. D., et al. "Economic Instability and Household Chaos Relate to Cortisol for Children in Poverty." *Journal of Family Psychology* 33, no. 6 (2019): 629–39.

Gao, A., and J. Jiang. "Perceived Empowering Leadership, Harmonious Passion, and Employee Voice: The Moderating Role of Job Autonomy." *Frontiers in Psychology* 10, no. 1484 (2019): 1–9.

Kuo, M., M. Barnes, and C. Jordan. "Do Experiences with Nature Promote Learning? Converging Evidence of a Cause-and-Effect Relationship." *Frontiers in Psychology* (2019), 1–9.

Pain, R., and T. Townsend. "A Safer City Centre for All? Senses of 'Community Safety' in Newcastle upon Tyne." *Geoforum* 33 (2002): 105–19.

Sarkar, A., and N. Garg. "Peaceful Workplace" only a Myth? Examining the Mediating Role of Psychological Capital on Spirituality and Nonviolence." *International Journal of Conflict Management* 31, no. 5 (2020): 709–28.

Weisner, T. "Well-Being, Chaos, and Culture: Sustaining a Meaningful Daily Routine. In *Chaos and Its Influence on Children's Development*. G. W. Evans and T. D. Wach, eds. Washington, D.C.: American Psychological Association, 2010.

Organized

Barrett, P., et al. "The Impact of Classroom Design on Pupils' Learning: Results of a Holistic, Multilevel Analysis." *School of the Built Environment, Building and Environment* 89 (2015): 118–33.

Cameron, C. E., et al. "Effects of Variation in Teacher Organization on Classroom Functioning." *Journal of School Psychology* 23 (2005): 61–85.

Froehlich, D., M. Segers, and P. Van den Bossche. "Informal Workplace Learning in Austrian Banks: The Influence of Learning Approach, Leadership Style, and Organizational Learning Culture on Managers' Learning Outcomes." *Human Resource Development Quarterly* 25, no. 1 (2014): 29–57.

Hauge, L. J., A. Skogstad, and S. Einarsen. "Relationships Between Stressful Work Environments and Bullying: Results of a Large Representative Study." *Work & Stress* 21, no. 3 (2007): 220–42.

Larsen, K. L., and S. S. Jordan. "Organized Chaos: Daily Routines Link Household Chaos and Child Behavior Problems. *Journal of Child and Family Studies* 29 (2020): 1094–1107.

Ponitz, C. C., et al. "Early Adjustment, Gender Differences, and Classroom Organizational Climate in First Grade." *Elementary School Journal* 110, no. 2 (2009): 142–62.

Respectful

Coelho, L., et al. "Quality of Play, Social Acceptance and Reciprocal Friendship in Preschool Children." *European Early Childhood Education Research Journal* 25, no. 6 (2017): 812–82.

Esbati, Z., and C. Korunka. "Does Intragroup Conflict Intensity Matter? The Moderating Effects of Conflict Management on Emotional Exhaustion and Work Engagement." *Frontiers in Psychology* 12 (2021): 1–15.

LaGree, D., et al. "The Effect of Respect: Respectful Communication at Work Drives Resiliency, Engagement, and Job Satisfaction Among Early Career Employees." *International Journal of Business Communication* (2021). Retrieved from https://journals.sagepub.com/doi/abs/10.1177/23294884211016529.

Miller, R., and J. Pedro. "Creating Respectful Classroom Environments." *Early Childhood Education Journal* 33, no. 5 (2006): 293–99.

Ng, T. W. G. "Embedding Employees Early On: The Importance of Workplace Respect." *Personnel Psychology* 69 (2016): 599–633.

Nossa, R., et al. "Engagement of Families Attending Early Childhood Services During 5-Month School Closure Due to COVID-19: An Italian Experience." *Frontiers in Psychology* 12 (2021): 1–9.

Part 5: Simple Rules for Learning Experiences

General

Freire, P. *Pedagogy of the Oppressed*. New York: Continuum, 1970.

Garau, C., and A. Annunziata. "Smart City Governance and Children's Agency: An Assessment of the Green Infrastructure Impact on Children's Activities in Cagliari (Italy) with the Tool 'Opportunities for Children in Urban Spaces (OCUS).'" *Sustainability* 11, no. 4848 (2019): 1–24.

MacFarquhar, L. "The Mind-Expanding Ideas of Andy Clark." *New Yorker*, March 26, 2018. https://www.newyorker.com/magazine/2018/04/02/the-mind-expanding-ideas-of-andy-clark.

Taylor, L., et al. "Teacher Educators' Apprenticeships of Observation and Community-Based Field Settings." *Frontiers in Education* 7(2022): 1–15.

Meaningful

Allan, B., et al. "Self-Determination, and Meaningful Work: Exploring Socioeconomic Constraints." *Frontiers in Psychology* 7, no. 71 (2016): 1–9.

Jeong, J., et al. "Parenting Interventions to Promote Early Child Development in the First Three Years of Life: A Global Systematic Review and Meta-Analysis." *PLOS Med* 18, no. 5 (2021): 1–51.

Johannsen, A., et al. 2012. "Enhancing Meaningful Learning and Self-Efficacy Through Collaboration Between Dental Hygienist and Physiotherapist Students: A Scholarship Project." *International Journal of Dental Hygiene* 10 (2012): 270–76.

Karpicke, J. D., and P. J. Grimaldi. "Retrieval-Based Learning: A Perspective for Enhancing Meaningful Learning." *Educational Psychology Review* 24 (2012): 401–18.

Polman, J., L. Hornstra, and M. Volman. "The Meaning of Meaningful Learning in Mathematics in Upper-Primary Education." *Learning Environments Research* 24 (2021): 469–86.

Exploratory

Evangleou, D., et al. "Talking about Artifacts: Preschool Children's Explorations with Sketches, Stories, and Tangible Objects." *Early Childhood Research and Practice* 12, no. 2 (2010). Retrieved from https://files.eric.ed.gov/fulltext/EJ910912.pdf.

Holzinger, A., et al. "Learning Performance with Interactive Simulations in Medical Education: Lessons Learned from Results of Learning Complex Physiological Models with the HAEMOdynamics SIMulator." *Computers & Education* 52 (2009): 292–301.

McGrath, R. G. 2001. "Exploratory Learning, Innovative Capacity, and Managerial Oversight." *Academy Of Management Journal* 44, no. 1 (2001): 118–31.

Muentener, P., E. Herrig, and L. Schulz. "The Efficiency of Infants Exploratory Play Is Related to Longer-Term Cognitive Development." *Frontiers in Psychology* 9, no. 635 (2018): 1–18.

Paddle, E., and J. Gilliland. "Orange Is the New Green: Exploring the Restorative Capacity of Seasonal Foliage in Schoolyard Trees." *International Journal of Environmental Research and Public Health* 13, no. 497 (2016): 1–18.

Actionable

Blewitt, C., et al. "'It's Embedded in What We Do for Every Child': A Qualitative Exploration of Early Childhood Educators' Perspectives on Supporting Children's Social and Emotional Learning." *International Journal of Environmental Research and Public Health*, 18, no. 1530 (2021): 1–16.

McCormick-Smith, M., and T. Chao. "Critical Science and Mathematics Early Childhood Education: Theorizing Reggio, Play, and Critical Pedagogy into an Actionable Cycle." *Education Sciences* 8, no. 162 (2018): 1–16.

Roth, G., and H. Bradbury. "Learning History: An Action Research Practice in Support of Actionable Learning. In *The SAGE Handbook of Action Research*. P. Reason and H. Bradbury, eds. Newbury Park, CA: SAGE Publications Ltd., 2011.

Part 6: Taking Action

Friedman-Krauss A. H., et al. 2014. "Child Behavior Problems, Teacher Executive Functions, and Teacher Stress in Head Start Classrooms." *Early Education and Development* 25, no. 5 (2014): 681–702.

Murray, D. W. "Self-Regulation and Toxic Stress: Foundations for Understanding Self-Regulation from an Applied Developmental Perspective." OPRE Report #2015-21. Washington, DC: Office of Planning, Research and Evaluation, Administration for Children and Families, U.S. Department of Health and Human Services, 2015.

Obama, Michelle. *Becoming*. New York: Random House, 2021.

Acknowledgments

Having an idea and turning it into a book is a fabulous process—extremely challenging and unequivocally collaborative! The idea for the 11 Simple Rules began with colleagues in Arkansas in 2016. Thank you to the Early Childhood Directors connected to Arkansas State University Childhood Services who affirmed Judy's suggestion that a much simpler way of thinking about early learning quality would improve their day-to-day work with teachers, children, and families. To Diana Courson and Jill Gunderman, we are grateful for your partnership and friendship.

Thanks to Laura Ensler, Gary Romano, and Joelle Gruber Wheatley who helped shape the initial concept of the Coherent Path to Quality into 11 Simple Rules. To Michael Luft and Andrew Davis, thank you for the inspiration you consistently offered as we shaped this project. We extend deep appreciation to our partners in Mississippi and Wyoming, Nikki Baldwin, Lauren Carlisle, April May, Kenecha Brooks-Smith, Marneshia Cathey, Nancy Sylvester, Leigh Sargent, Cheryl Swoopes, and Amy Donaldson, who believe in Leading for Children and how the Learning Network approach can bring equity, cohesion, and quality to early learning in your states. We will be forever grateful to the members of Mississippi Leadership for Children and the Wyoming Quality Learning Network for the wisdom they shared.

Thank you to all the educators with whom we've had the privilege of partnering over many years. Your wisdom is inspirational. We extend sincere gratitude to Holly Seplocha, Katherine Schneider, Christine Shrader Ast, Cailyn Lynn, Serene Stevens, and Jonathan Fribley for sharing stories from their experience to help illustrate each of the simple rules.

Our thinking about why each rule matters has been enriched by our stellar research team led by Sarah Zawacki with support from Keyonna Hayes, Jeanne Hanna, and Jonathan Fribley. We are grateful for your contributions to this book.

To the amazing photographers who have contributed to the richness and beauty of this book, our sincerest thanks to all of you: Amber Jones, Barbra Blender, Gabriel Guyton, Gretchen Stack, Jahari Bell, Julie Nichols, Kathie Autumn, Kenecha Brooks-Smith, LaTanya Bennett, Nichole Parks, Rachel Swanson, Tanya Taylor, and Tara Skiles. Vik Gupta, thank you for your magnificent photo that invites readers into our book. Jamie Wenger and Angela Dutton, your persistence, talents, and humor bring together the photographic story of the 11 Simple Rules.

We appreciate the assistance of our terrific editorial team, Hope Matthiessen and Jane Cavolina. The invaluable insights of many of our LFC team, friends, family, and colleagues offered guidance along the way: Gracie Parks, Shannon Newman, Abasi Clark, Lara Galinsky, Erica Hamilton, Erin Murphy, Ahmed Yearwood, Frank Liu, Thomas Palatucci, and Anders Cato, your knowledge and patience support us every day. Angela Corbo Gier, you dazzle us with your wisdom, humor, and talent as you transform our ideas into a beautiful book.

Gretchen Henderson, you never waver in your encouragement and persistence every step of the way! Lisa Holton, you are our north star! Without your remarkable steadiness, brilliance, and love, we would still be talking about the idea of this book.

We know how fortunate we are to have life mates—Wilbert and Andy—who make every day of our lives a treasure. And to each other, we say, thanks for being the great dance partners. How lucky we are to have one another as the very best colleagues and friends.

About the Authors

Judy Jablon is the founder and Executive Director of Leading for Children, a national non-profit organization. After having spent over forty years in the field of early learning, Judy has developed a groundbreaking model that focuses on community and the collective wisdom of its members. Her work centers around the great passion and determination of all the different individuals who dedicate their lives to leading for children. Judy is the author of numerous books and resources for the field including *Powerful Interactions: How to Connect with Children to Extend Their Learning*, and *The Five Commitments of Optimistic Leaders: A Reflective Practice Journal*. Judy began Leading for Children in 2016 to focus on equity in early learning by ensuring that all the adults in the young child's ecosystem can come together to collectively solve the challenges of their communities by using their wisdom and experience. LFC's projects are currently under way in more than ten states across the country.

Nichole Parks is the Director of Programs at Leading for Children. Her philosophy is that by nurturing the growth and development of the adults in the child's ecosystem, we create pathways to sustainable quality and take steps to create a more equitable world for our children. During her twenty-nine years in early childhood education, she's taught preschool and served children and families as the Infant and Toddler Director of NAEYC accredited program. Prior to joining LFC she was the Quality Rating Improvement System Coordinator with Arkansas State University Childhood Services, where she coordinated trainings, coaching, assessments, and initiatives for early childhood program administrators. Nichole has developed place-based resources in several states and is a co-author of *The Five Commitments of Optimistic Leaders: A Reflective Practice Journal*.